Leaves

by Gail Saunders-Smith

Photo: Yellow Ladyslipper

Content Consultant:
Deborah Brown, Horticulturist
University of Minnesota Extension Service

Pebble Books

an imprint of Capstone Press

Pebble Books

Pebble Books are published by Capstone Press
818 North Willow Street, Mankato, Minnesota 56001
http://www.capstone-press.com

Library of Congress Cataloging-in-Publication Data
Saunders-Smith, Gail.
    Leaves/by Gail Saunders-Smith
        p. cm.
    Includes bibliographical references (p. 23) and index.
    Summary: Describes the different sizes and shapes of leaves, the function of chlorophyll, and
the process of photosynthesis using simple text and illustrations.
    ISBN 1-56065-770-7
    1. Leaves--Juvenile literature. [1. Leaves.] I. Title.
    QK649.S265 1998
    575.5'7--dc21   98-5046
                                                                                     CIP
                                                                                      AC

Note to Parents and Teachers

This book describes and illustrates information about leaves, including sizes
and shapes, chlorophyll, and photosynthesis. The close picture-text matches
support early readers in understanding the text. The text offers subtle
challenges with compound and complex sentence structures. This book also
introduces early readers to expository and content-specific vocabulary. The
expository vocabulary is defined in the Words to Know section. Early readers
may need assistance in reading some of these words. Readers also may need
assistance in using the Table of Contents, Words to Know, Read More, Internet
Sites and Index/Word List sections of the book.

Table of Contents

Plants have leaves. Leaves make food for plants. They make food from air and sunlight.

Leaves grow from the stems of plants. The flat part of a leaf is the blade. The blade takes in air and sunlight.

Photo: Begonia Leaf

Leaves can be many shapes and sizes. Leaves can be thick or thin. They can be long or short. They can be narrow or wide.

Photo: Water Lily

Leaves grow at the bottoms of stems on some plants. Leaves grow on the sides of stems on other plants. Leaves can grow in bunches, or they can alternate. Alternate is to take turns. Alternating leaves grow one at a time up the sides of a stem.

Photo: Tulips

Leaves have veins. A vein is like a tiny pipe. Veins carry water and food. Veins bring water from the stems to the leaves. Veins also take food made by the leaves to the stems.

14

Leaves also have cells. The cells take in water and air. Chlorophyll is inside the cells. Chlorophyll makes most leaves look green.

Chlorophyll uses sunlight to turn water and carbon dioxide into food. Carbon dioxide is a gas in the air. Leaves take in carbon dioxide. People breathe out carbon dioxide.

Photo: Sunflower

Photosynthesis is the action of leaves making food. Leaves give off oxygen during photosynthesis. People breathe in oxygen.

Food made during photosynthesis travels down the veins to the stem. The stem carries this food to other parts of the plant.

Words to Know

alternate—to take turns

carbon dioxide—a gas in the air; plants take in carbon dioxide, and people breathe out carbon dioxide

chlorophyll—something leaves make that makes them look green; chlorophyll uses sunlight to turn water and carbon dioxide into food

narrow—a short way across; not wide

oxygen—a gas in the air; people breathe in oxygen, and plants give off oxygen

photosynthesis—the action of plants using chlorophyll and sunlight to turn water and carbon dioxide into food

stem—the long part of a plant that grows above ground; leaves and flowers grow from the stem

vein—a small tube or pipe inside a leaf; veins carry water and food through a plant

22

Read More

Barlowe, Dot. *Learning about Leaves.* Mineola, N.Y.: Dover Publications Inc., 1997.

Bryant-Mole, Karen. *Flowers.* Austin, Tex.: Raintree Steck-Vaughn, 1996.

Fowler, Allan. *It Could Still Be a Leaf.* Chicago: Children's Press, 1995.

Internet Sites

Common Wildflowers
http://www.tpwd.state.tx.us/adv/kidspage/kidquiz/wildflwr/wildflwr.htm

4-H Children's Garden
http://commtechlab.msu.edu/sites/garden/index.html

Photosynthesis
http://ericir.syr.edu/Projects/Newton/9/phytosy.html

Index/Word List

air, 5, 7, 15, 17
blade, 7
carbon dioxide, 17
cells, 15
chlorophyll, 15, 17
food, 5, 13, 17, 19, 21
gas, 17
green, 15
leaves, 5, 7, 9, 11, 13, 15,
    17, 19
oxygen, 19

people, 17, 19
photosynthesis, 19, 21
pipe, 13
plant, 5, 7, 11, 21
shapes, 9
sizes, 9
stems, 7, 11, 13, 21
sunlight, 5, 7, 17
vein, 13, 21
water, 13, 15, 17

Word Count: 236
Early-Intervention Reading Level: 11

Editorial Credits
Lois Wallentine, editor; James Franklin, design; Michelle L. Norstad, photo research

Photo Credits
Dembinsky Photo Associates/Bill Lea, 1; Ron Planek, 8; Michael Hubrich, 10; Stan Osolinski, 20
William B. Folsom, 18
Dwight Kuhn, 14
Kay Shaw, 4
James P. Rowan, cover
Doris Van Buskirk, 6, 12, 16